RESOLVING CONFLICT

BY ABBY COLICH

BLUE OWL
BOOKS

TIPS FOR CAREGIVERS

Social and emotional learning (SEL) helps children manage emotions, learn how to feel empathy, create and achieve goals, and make good decisions. Strong lessons and support in SEL will help children establish positive habits in communication, cooperation, and decision-making. By incorporating SEL in early reading, children will learn the importance of resolving conflict when working with others.

BEFORE READING

Talk to the reader about conflict. Give examples of conflict. Ask the reader to think about times he or she has experienced conflicts.

Discuss: When was a time you had a conflict? What happened? How was it resolved?

AFTER READING

Talk to the reader about the importance of communication in resolving conflict.

Discuss: What are some ways you can prevent and resolve conflict with your words?

SEL GOAL

Children may have a difficult time understanding that everyone experiences conflict at one time or another and that some conflicts can be easily resolved. Role-play different scenarios involving conflict. Have readers practice what they would say aloud. Remind readers that conflict can often be easily resolved, and moving forward can help them feel better.

TABLE OF CONTENTS

CHAPTER 1

WHAT IS CONFLICT?

When you work in a group, you get to spend time with others. You learn from each other, too. But at times, you will experience **conflict**.

Conflict can happen when people don't agree. It can also happen when something goes wrong. But you can work to prevent and **resolve** conflict. It just takes some **teamwork** and **communication**.

CHAPTER 2

PREVENTING CONFLICT

One way to prevent conflict is to be **patient**. Erin says she doesn't like Tyler's idea for their project. Tyler wants to talk back right away. But he takes a deep breath. He thinks about a nice way to respond.

Bella and Harry are building a robot. Harry doesn't understand the instructions. Bella stays patient. She shows **empathy**. She tells Harry she was confused at first, too. She helps explain the steps.

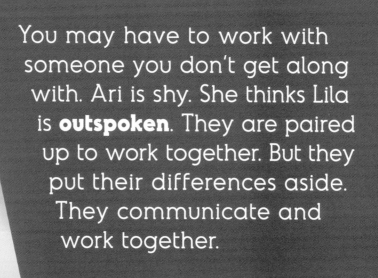

You may have to work with someone you don't get along with. Ari is shy. She thinks Lila is **outspoken**. They are paired up to work together. But they put their differences aside. They communicate and work together.

SHARED GOALS

If you don't get along with a group member, remember that you have the same **goals**. You both want to finish your project and do a good job.

Communicate with your group. Listen to others. This helps make sure you all understand one another.

Beau wants to change part of a group presentation. But he asks his teammates first. He listens to their **opinions**.

DO YOU AGREE?

When you think your group has come to a decision about something, make sure everyone agrees on it. How? Try repeating the decision using different words.

CHAPTER 3

FINDING SOLUTIONS

Conflict can make you feel angry or upset. Stop and take a deep breath. You may need to take a break. Try going on a short walk.

Sometimes our **emotions** take over. Be **mindful** of the situation. Write down your thoughts. Try to focus on the group's goals.

Talk through the conflict with your group members. Listen to their opinions about what happened. Make sure you all understand and agree on what the problem is. Then you can figure out what caused it. Knowing the cause can help prevent conflict in the future.

TAKE OWNERSHIP

Take **ownership** for your part in the conflict. How? Say sorry if you think you were wrong about something or if you made a mistake.

/ DOM
language = 'JavaScript'>
document.write ("Hello World");
<a href ="http://

</CENTER>
text=

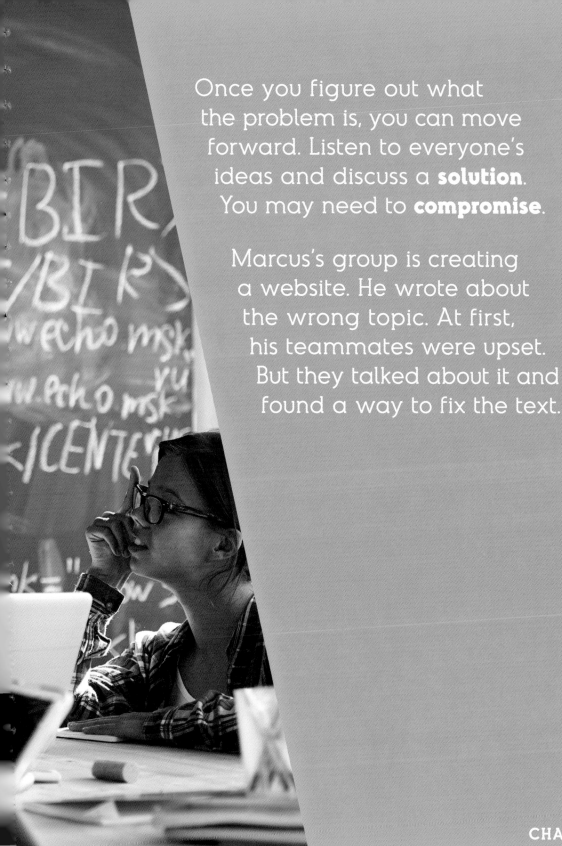

Once you figure out what the problem is, you can move forward. Listen to everyone's ideas and discuss a **solution**. You may need to **compromise**.

Marcus's group is creating a website. He wrote about the wrong topic. At first, his teammates were upset. But they talked about it and found a way to fix the text.

If you don't like the way things turned out, try to be a good sport. Maya isn't happy with her group's decision. They decided to do a skit for their history project. She wanted to make a poster instead. But she tells her group that she understands the decision. She says, "I know where everyone is coming from. Maybe next time we can try my idea."

When conflict happens, you can learn from it. Dealing with conflict can help you learn to communicate better. You might be able to prevent the same problem from happening again.

When you and your team members know how to prevent and resolve conflict, you can accomplish more!

GOALS AND TOOLS

GROW WITH GOALS

Everyone experiences conflict at some point. Knowing how to handle it can help you come to a solution and prevent it in the future.

Goal: Speak up if you see conflict happening or about to happen in your group. Help your teammates figure out what the problem is. Discuss a solution.

Goal: Keep your emotions in check. Try not to react too quickly. Think about what you want to say before you say it.

Goal: Reflect on conflict after it happens. Think about lessons you learned. Consider what went well when you were coming to a solution.

WRITING REFLECTION

Take time to reflect on how you have handled conflict in the past. Think about how you might handle it in the future.

1. Write about a time you experienced conflict while working with others. How was it resolved? Is there anything you wish you had done differently?

2. Make a list of phrases you can use to help reach a solution. Ask a trusted adult for suggestions if you're stuck.

3. Write about a lesson you learned from a conflict you experienced. How might this experience help you during a future conflict?

GLOSSARY

communication
The sharing of information, ideas, or feelings with another person through language, eye contact, or gestures.

compromise
To agree to accept something that is not entirely what you wanted in order to satisfy some of the requests of other people.

conflict
A serious, lengthy disagreement.

emotions
Feelings, such as happiness, anger, or sadness.

empathy
The ability to understand and be sensitive to the thoughts and feelings of others.

goals
Things you aim to do.

mindful
A mentality achieved by focusing on the present moment and calmly recognizing and accepting your feelings, thoughts, and sensations.

opinions
Personal feelings or beliefs.

outspoken
Very honest and direct, especially when criticizing someone or something.

ownership
The state or fact of owning something.

patient
Able to put up with problems or delays without getting angry or upset.

resolve
To find a solution to a problem or to settle a difficulty.

solution
An answer or means to solving a problem.

teamwork
The work done by a group of people who accomplish something together.

TO LEARN MORE

FACT SURFER

Finding more information is as easy as 1, 2, 3.

1. Go to www.factsurfer.com

2. Enter "**resolvingconflict**" into the search box.

3. Choose your book to see a list of websites.

INDEX

Blue Owl Books are published by Jump!, 5357 Penn Avenue South, Minneapolis, MN 55419, www.jumplibrary.com

Copyright © 2022 Jump! International copyright reserved in all countries. No part of this book may be reproduced in any form without written permission from the publisher.

Library of Congress Cataloging-in-Publication Data

Names: Colich, Abby, author.
Title: Resolving conflict / Abby Colich.
Description: Minneapolis: Jump!, Inc., 2022. | Series: Working together | Includes index. | Audience: Ages 7–10
Identifiers: LCCN 2021008057 (print)
LCCN 2021008058 (ebook)
ISBN 9781636901237 (hardcover)
ISBN 9781636901244 (paperback)
ISBN 9781636901251 (ebook)
Subjects: LCSH: Problem solving—Juvenile literature. | Interpersonal conflict—Juvenile literature. | Conflict management—Juvenile literature.
Classification: LCC BF449 .C65 2022 (print)
LCC BF449 (ebook) | DDC 153.4/3—dc23
LC record available at https://lccn.loc.gov/2021008057
LC ebook record available at https://lccn.loc.gov/2021008058

Editor: Eliza Leahy
Designer: Molly Ballanger

Photo Credits: Shutterstock, cover; wavebreakmedia/Shutterstock, 1; sunabesyou/Shutterstock, 3; Alina555/iStock, 4l; Image bug/Shutterstock, 4r; SDI Productions/iStock, 5; Kazutoshi Kikuchi/iStock, 6; monkeybusinessimages/iStock, 7; FatCamera/iStock, 8–9; jlmatt/iStock, 10–11; Ljupco/iStock, 12; Marco VDM/iStock, 13; SeventyFour/Shutterstock, 14–15; mediaphotos/iStock, 16–17; adamkaz/iStock, 18–19; kali9/iStock, 20–21.

Printed in the United States of America at Corporate Graphics in North Mankato, Minnesota.